The Dominicans

The Dominicans

Letters to a Young Man on the Dominican Order

PÈRE PAUL DUCHAUSSOY, O.P.

Translated by
Bede Jarrett, O.P.

Edited by
The Very Rev. Father John Procter, S. T. M.
Provincial of the English Dominicans

AROUCA
PRESS

Published in cooperation with
The O.P. Prayer Apostolate.
https://www.op-prayer.com

Originally published by
R. & T. Washbourne, LTD., 1909.

ISBN: 978-1-990685-98-9

Arouca Press
PO Box 55003
Bridgeport PO
Waterloo, ON N2J 0A5
Canada
www.aroucapress.com
Send inquiries to info@aroucapress.com

Nihil Obstat.
Fr. PETRUS READER, O.P., M.A.
Fr. VICENTIUS McNABB, O.P., S.T.L.

Imprimatur.
✠ GULIIELMUS
Episcopus Arindelensis,
Vicarius Generalis.
Westmonasterii,
Die 4 Feb., 1909.

Contents

Editor's Note

THE O.P. PRAYER APOSTOLATE WAS founded in August of 2021 with the aim of preserving the beautiful spirituality, charism, and liturgy of the Order of Preachers, as well as promoting vocations to the Order, through the means of the internet and, now, through the publication of this book, which I truly believe will become a classic of Dominican literature.

In this book, you will read the letters of a holy priest to a young man discerning a vocation to the Order of Preachers, which answers his questions about the history of the Order, the prayer of the Order, and the struggles which come with accepting such a life.

I pray that this book may bring you ever closer to Almighty God and to the Holy Order under His Mother's Patronage.

CALDER CLAYDON
Founder, O. P. Prayer Apostolate

Foreword

THE FOLLOWING PAGES ON ST. DOMI-
nic and his spirit, as embodied in the Order
which he founded, were written in the form
of letters—and there are ten of them—to an
inquiring young friend, by the Very Rev. Père
Duchaussoy, O.P.[1] With his kind permission,
they have been translated from the French, in
which they were originally written, by the Rev.
Fr. Bede Jarrett , B.A., S.T.L., of the same Order.

To these letters another—as an appen-
dix—has been added, at my suggestion, by
the pen of a Sister of the Congregation of
Siena, whose motherhouse is at Stone, on the
life, spirit, and work of the nuns of the Second and Third Orders, the first-born children
of St. Dominic. A Chapter will also be found
on Tertiaries living in the world.

A few editorial notes have also been added.
It is hoped that this brochure will meet a long

---

1 *Les Dominicains:* Lettres à un jeune homme sur l'Ordre
des Frères Prêcheurs (quatri me edition).

felt want in the Dominican literature of the three English-speaking Provinces, answering, as it does, briefly and succinctly, certain questions often put to the members of the Order of both sexes in the three countries in which the English tongue prevails.

St. Dominic's Priory,
JOHN PROCTER, O.P.
Haverstock Hill, London, N. W.

LETTER I
The Life of St. Dominic

OF COURSE, WHAT YOU WILL first of all want to ask is, What sort of a man was the founder of our Order? And then, What was his object in instituting the Friars Preachers?

Our Holy Father was, as you know, St. Dominic. He was born at Calaroga, a little town in Spain, in the year of Our Lord 1170. His father, Felix de Gusman, and his mother, Joan d'Aza, were both nobly born, and to their noble birth added the greater gift of nobler virtue. The birth of our Saint was preceded by a sign that has since become famous. His mother saw in her dream the fruit of her womb in the form of a dog; in its mouth gleamed a bright-burning torch, with which it seemed to set the world alight.

Again, when he was taken as a child to the font, his god-mother saw on his brow a brilliant, star-like radiance, foretelling anew the greatness that would attend his steps.

It was in his mother's arms that Dominic
lived in infancy, nourished by her, watched and
protected by her, taught by her the prayers
of childhood, and learning from her lips the
fruits of faith. As a boy he left his mother
and his home, and went to live with his uncle,
the Archpriest of Izan. Here, under the dou-
ble authority of blood-relationship and of the
priesthood, he grew in knowledge and in those
graces of stately courtesy for which the Spanish nobility are still so famous. Then, when he
was sent to Palencia, to follow at that University the customary scholastic lectures in all the
branches of medieval knowledge. He entered
on this new life at the age of fifteen and for
the next ten years remained there, pursuing
his studies with all that characteristic ardour
for which Dante has spoken of him as "the
hallowed wrestler" or under another metaphor
as "like torrent bursting from a lofty vein."

At first he would probably have followed
the schools of literature and philosophy. "But,"
says a chronicler, "though easily mastering all
human science, he was not led captive by it,
for he found not there God's Wisdom, which
is Christ; therefore turned he to his Master,
praying that his heart might be opened to true
knowledge and his ears attuned to the teach-
ings of Holy Writ. So sweet was this Divine

Word to him, so eagerly did he receive it, that he passed his nights often without sleep, giving to study the time he took from rest. His whole life, indeed, was spent in diligent prayer, and in study no wit less diligent."

At the age of twenty-five he was ordained priest, vowing his life to the service of God, among the Canons Regular of Osma. The Prior of the Chapter was at the time Dom Diego, eventually Bishop of the same See. "Then," says Blessed Jordan of Saxony (1190–1237), "he appeared among his brethren, the Canons, as a shining light, foremost in holiness, in his own estimation lowliest, breathing around him a life-giving odour and a perfume like sweet-smelling frankincense in the summer time."

For nine years he lived at Osma, preparing himself unconsciously for the great work which God would have him to do.

In 1203, Dominic left Spain and crossed over into France. Apparently and in outward seeming his purpose was to accompany his Bishop, Dom Diego, on a political mission to Denmark, to negotiate some matter on behalf of the King of Castile. Really he was being led by the providence of God to his place of destiny. He came into the country of Toulouse, then ravaged by the terrible Albigensian heresy. Here his first work was to bring back to the faith the heretic who had given him hospitality. In that moment Dominic had found his calling: it was to convert souls to God by the ministry of preaching. Yet even now God asked of him twelve more years of preparation. Those twelve years were spent in a fashion of life as strenuous as that of the first Apostles. He preached in season and out of season, exhorting, rebuking, consoling, encouraging. He taught on every side the truths of faith, so that the poor might have once more the Gospel preached to them. The institution of the Rosary, in whatever form it may have originated, dates, according to the tradition of the Popes, from these years of missionary labour. Miracles and prophecies confirmed the doctrine that he expounded.

At last, in the forty-sixth year of a life that was to be complete in its fifty-first, St. Dominic gathered together a few companions, laid the foundations of his Order, and went to Rome to ask for the blessing of the Sovereign Pontiff on his work. Here visions from on high encouraged and confirmed him in his generous ambitions. He it was whom Our Lady offered to her Son as a devoted and intrepid captain who would marshal his hosts to make war on sin and error.

He it was whom St. Peter and St. Paul proclaimed to be chosen by God to preach; for one day as he knelt in prayer in the old basilica of St. Peter's, the two Prince-Apostles appeared to him, the one giving him a staff, the other a book, saying to him together: "Go thou and preach, for unto this art thou called."

Trained in the religious life, and accustomed to the fasts, abstinences, watchings, and other observances contained in the rule of St. Benedict, St. Dominic took them all over, almost as they stood, for his own Order. To these he added the rule of St. Augustine, producing a short compendium of constitutions for the use of his children.

In 1215, Pope Innocent III, learning by a vision from God that St. Dominic and his brethren would become the defenders of the Church and be numbered among her brightest luminaries, decided to approve our Holy Father's project of founding an Order destined for preaching. His successor, Honorius III, on December 22 in the year following, officially confirmed the Order in all its rules and constitutions, granting to its members by his supreme authority the privilege of preaching and hearing confessions wheresoever they would.

The following is a translation of a Bull addressed to our Holy Father the same day:

Honorius, servant of the servants of God, to his dear son Dominic, and to the brethren who have made or shall make profession of the regular life, health and Apostolic Benediction:

"Considering that the religious of your Order will be the champions of the faith and the true lights of the world, We confirm your Order, with all its lands and possessions, present and future, and We take beneath Our care and protection the Order itself, together with all its possessions and privileges.

"Given at Rome at Sancta Sabina, the eleventh day before the Kalends of January, one thousand two hundred and sixteen, in the first year of Our Pontificate."

The Order of St. Dominic is founded at last. Let us now describe its wonderful success.[2]

---

2 The English Province begun by Gilbert de Fresnoy in 1221, which at first included Ireland and Scotland as vicariates, could show 40 priories in 1277, which rose to 87 by the year 1303. These three Provinces have produced six Cardinals and more than 140 Bishops. The Province of the United States dates from the early part of the last century, and numbers at present nearly 200 members.

LETTER II
St. Dominic's Aim and Object

"IN THREE OR FOUR MONTHS,"
says Lacordaire, "St. Dominic had gathered together at St. Sixtus as many as a hundred religious. The slowness of action that
had hitherto characterized him was succeeded
by a marked rapidity. He had only begun his
career at the age of thirty-five, and he had
spent twelve further years in forming sixteen
disciples. Now, however, he saw them falling
at his feet as falls the ripe grain before the
reaper's scythe. There is nothing paradoxical
in this; for it is a law no less of Nature than
of grace that a force long pent-up acts with
the greater impetuosity as long as its cramping
barriers are removed. In everything there is
a point which, once attained, renders success
prompt and inevitable. Never did Dominic show
clearer manifestations of the power God had
given him; never did Nature render him more
obedient reverence. This was the triumphant
moment of his life."

Miracles follow quickly in the pages of the chroniclers of his life. One time the roof of his first priory falls in and buries a labourer in its ruins. Dominic hurries up to the spot, prays to Him Who refuses nothing to the prayer of faith, and life and health return to the mangled remains that lie before him. Another time the poor friars are left without food. At the wonted hour he orders the bell to be rung for supper. He enters the refectory, followed by the community. They recite their grace as joyfully as ever, and seat themselves on the little narrow benches.

St. Dominic prays. Lo! Two angels clothed in white appear, and, beginning at the lowest end of the refectory, on right and left, they place before each brother a loaf of bread of marvellous beauty. One morning our Holy Father is in consultation with some Cardinals on the needs of the Order. Suddenly a man breaks in upon them, and, with violent signs of grief, cries out that Cardinal Stephen's nephew has just died, killed by a fall from his horse. Dominic starts up, runs to the place of the accident, has the body taken into a room apart, and prepares to say his Mass. When he has completed the Holy Sacrifice, he turns to the corpse, and there, in the presence of the Cardinals and of his brethren, he says in a loud voice: "Young man, I say to thee, in the

Name of Our Lord Jesus Christ, arise." At once the young man gets up, and St. Dominic gives him back in joy to his uncle, the Cardinal.[3]

Souls could not resist the eloquence of our Saint. Some gave up their evil habits, living good Christian lives among their fellows. Others, fired with a nobler ardour, asked to enter into the cloister. Within five years St. Dominic had founded sixty priories, peopled with picked men of genius or with youths who gave promise of equal intellectual gifts. The second Master-General, Jordan of Saxony, gave the black-and-white habit to more than a thousand postulants whom he had himself attracted to this new manner of life. The work then was accomplished. The worker was needed no longer. He could go to his Master and receive his promised reward.

On August 6, 1221, in the fifty-fifth year of his age, St. Dominic died at Bologna. He was canonized in 1234 by Gregory IX, who is said to have declared that he no more doubted of the holiness of St. Dominic than he did of the Apostles Peter and Paul. He speaks of him in the Bull of Canonization as one,

3 In grateful thanks the Cardinal gave to the Dominican Convent of St. Sixtus the yearly rent of 50 marks out of the revenues of the parish church of Bambrough, in Northumberland. In 1428 land in Italy and 3,086 florins of gold were given in place of it.

who grew in grace even as he grew
in years; and so zealous was he for
the salvation of souls that, not con-
tent with devoting himself wholly to
the work of preaching, he enlisted
such numbers beneath his own banner that he has won a name and place
for himself among the patriarchs. A
prince and shepherd among God's
people, he instituted a new Order of
Preachers, guided it by his example, and confirmed it by his miracles.
We who knew him intimately in the
days when We filled a less exalted
office in the Church, who saw in his
life an evident proof of his holiness,
now that witnesses worthy of credit
have attested to the truth of his miracles—We, together with the flock
the Lord has instructed to Our care,
believe that, thanks to the mercy of
God, he may aid Us by his powerful
prayers, and, after having consoled Us
on earth by his loving friendship, will
help us with his patronage in Heaven.

And now, how did we come by this title of
Preachers? It is the name given us by Innocent III. Having one day occasion to write
to St. Dominic, he told his secretary to put
this inscription: "To Brother Dominic and
his companions." Correcting himself, he said:
"Write it thus—'To Brother Dominic and

those who preach with him.'" Finally, after a
moment's reflection, he said: "No; put it this
way—'To Master Dominic and his preaching
brethren.'" Thenceforward St. Dominic himself
and his sons called themselves Friars Preachers, and by this name were they known at
the Roman Court and elsewhere.[4] This name,
given by Innocent III, approved by Honorius
III, and confirmed by Gregory IX, was surely
won long before by St. Dominic's prayers and
tears, and the fullness of his merits before
God. And truly our Order can and ought to
be called the Order of Friars Preachers, see-
ing that it was especially founded for the
saving of souls by preaching, according to the
very words with which the Book of the Constitutions opens: *Ordo noster specialiter ob
predicationem et salutem animarum ab initio
noscitur institutus.*

This, then, was the object of St. Dominic,
whom the Church honours under the titles
of *Lumen ecclesiae, doctor Veritatis*: to save
souls by preaching, to enlighten the world, to
convert heretics, to bring back sinners to God
from every land, savage or civilized. He came,

4 Over the white habit of the Dominicans a black cloak
and hood is worn in public and during winter. Hence in
England they were formerly known as Black Friars. Black-
friars in London is so called from the ancient Dominican
House there.

indeed, to found an Order of Apostles. "Pray ye therefore the Lord of the harvest, that He may send labourers into the harvest" (Matt. 9:38). How fervently throughout his life he prayed this prayer to God! And of what sort were the apostles whom he prayed to have sent him?

He wished for men who had left all things—left wealth and home and family—who could say to the Master, "Behold, we have left all things"; for men ever ready to go whithersoever their Superiors desired them to go—"Go ye into the whole world"; for men who would spend themselves and be spent in defence of the Church and the Holy See, even as the Pope had seen in vision our Holy Father himself supporting the tottering walls of the Lateran basilica; for men formed to this work of the apostolate by study, by silence, by contemplation joined to vocal recitation of the Divine Office, by a life of austerity and penance that would include all the monastic observances, such as the perpetual abstinence from flesh-meat within their convent walls (except in case of sickness of feebleness), the long fast from the Feast of the Holy Cross on September 14 up to Easter, the midnight rising to chant or recite Matins and Lauds. Such were the men for whom St. Dominic wished, religious apostles, Friars Preachers. This is the Order he founded, the Order he prayed for to God, the Order for which he obtained the approbation of the Church.

LETTER III
The Teachers in the Order

NATURALLY ENOUGH, AFTER what I have said, you will be inclined to ask whether the Order of Friars Preachers did correspond to the wishes of St. Dominic and the hopes of the Church. This, in turn, as far as the wishes of St. Dominic are concerned, subdivides into two other questions: Has the Order achieved the object for which he founded it? If it has done so, has it done it by the means which he desired?

Now, I have already remarked that our Holy Father's wish was to found an Order of apostles. But what is an apostle? Surely, an apostle is one who brings truth to souls. Consequently an Order of apostles must be first of all an Order of teachers. Now, before a man can bring truth to others, he must have it himself; before a lamp gives light, it must burn. Therefore a true apostle, a true teacher, must be one who knows the truth, who eagerly pursues it, who incessantly studies it. So well did the Friars

Preachers understand this that within a century of their founder's death they had acquired the title of the Order of Truth.

Now, what are the sources of truth?

The first is Holy Writ. It is by this that God has made manifest to man His truths and His will. It is by this that He has made His light to enlighten every eye, just as it is by this also that He has shown His love to every heart. It is, then, to this centre of light and love that an apostle should bring his mind to be illuminated and his heart to be set on fire. The study of Holy Writ is the first study of a true apostle; and so quite naturally, we find in our Order a great zeal for this sublime yet simple science. We have seen St. Dominic consecrating his nights to the study of true wisdom, which is Christ; and tradition tells us that in his journeyings he had with him but two books—the Gospel of St. Matthew, and the Epistles of St. Paul.

When, therefore, Dominican schools were founded, the chair of Holy Scripture was always looked upon as the most important. The translation of the inspired books from Hebrew, Syriac, and Greek was always included in the course of our universities.

Two works come prominently forward, and show the interest taken by the Order in the

Word of God. The first is the many attempts at correcting the Sacred Scriptures.

Witness the decree of the General Chapter of 1236, which commands that all the Bibles in the Order are to be corrected according to the exemplar revised by the friars of the Province of France. Witness also the labourers of Cardinal Hugh of St. Cher at the same task, of which eight manuscripts survive. Witness the labour of Xantes Pagninus, O. P., the first since St. Jerome to translate the entire Bible from the original languages.

The Order also took up as specially its own another enterprise, less scientific, no doubt, but not less laborious. This was the work of composing a concordance of the Bible. Hugh of St. Cher, the first Dominican Cardinal, took up the idea, already, indeed, roughly executed, of arranging every word of the Bible in alphabetical order.[5] The result was, of course, extremely useful for all preachers and professors, who had merely to turn up a single word, and find there, without any difficulty, every passage in the whole of the Scriptures where it occurred.

---

5 This concordance was afterwards amplified by three English Dominicans, John of Derlington, Richard of Stavensby, and Hugh of Croydon, so as to include in each reference not the word only, but each entire phrase in which the word is to be found. The copy still extant in Paris is said to be in Stavensby's own handwriting.

Again, Augostino Giustiani was the first to
inaugurate public lectures in Hebrew. This
he did at Paris, where he produced the whole
Bible as an *Octopla*, including the sacred text
in Latin, Greek, Hebrew, Chaldaic, and Arabic.
Biblical archaeology owes a great debt to Raymund Martini, the founder of modern biblical
orientalism, the greatest glory of those schools
for the study of Eastern languages founded by
St. Raymund Pennafort. He could speak and
write fluently Hebrew, Chaldaic, and Arabic.
His *Pugio Fidei* (1250) was a magnificent apol-
ogy for the New Testament—the first of its
kind—drawn from Talmudic writings. No less
is the debt which yet remains unpaid to Ric-
coldo da Montecroce, who inaugurated biblical
ethnology in his *Itinerarium;* and to Johann
Michael Wansleben, who originated the science
of Egyptology.

But the sacred Scriptures are not the only
source of truth. They give us, indeed, the prin-
ciples of truth, but do not always draw out
the conclusions. For this purpose there is a
science which we call theology or divinity. It
bases itself on revelation and further deduces
from these revealed truths other truths which
follow from them. Now, to mention the word
"theology" is to call up from the past the whole
of Dominican history since the day that St.

Dominic was created Master of the Sacred Palace and officially theologian of the Pope. It brings back to the mind the great schools of Paris, Bologna, and Oxford, of Montpellier, Salamanca, and Cologne. It conjures up the names of men held in reverence today, even by those who do not accept their methods or their conclusions. Such, for example, was that philosopher of the thirteenth century whom men called "the miracle of Nature" and "the wonder of his time," whom posterity has given the title of Albert *the Great*. Around him moved a host of brilliant disciples; among them is one whose radiance far outshines the rest in glory—our revered master and our well-loved brother, Thomas of Aquino.

To recite merely the titles of honour given him by the Sovereign Pontiffs would be to cover more pages than are to be found in this book. He is called the "sweet Psalmist of the Eucharist," "the Angelic Doctor," "the Angel of the Schools." He swept up and gathered into a single whole the scattered fragments of theology. Well known are the words of Pope John XXII, who, speaking of the articles into which the Summa is divided, said, Quot scripsit articulos, tot fecit miracula; or, again, the too proud boast of the apostate Bucer, "Take away St. Thomas, and I will destroy the Church—*Tolle Thomam*

et dissipabo Ecclesiam; or the nobler praise of
the Council of Trent which placed his Summa
by the side of the Scriptures and the works
of St. Augustine on the table in the council
chamber. But more eloquent than all are the
words of Leo XIII, to whom the Order of Friars
Preachers owes an everlasting debt of gratitude
for the affectionate manner in which he protected the theories and methods of St. Thomas.
"In him," said this Pope, "were all the highest
gifts of nature and of grace, whose life, no less
than his writings, is an example to the world:
fertile was he in reasoning, free from error,
marshalling his thoughts in wondrous order,
reverently submissive to faith, ever in tune with
the transcendent mysteries of revealed truth,
perfect in the manner of his living, shining with
the adornment of every virtue." (But cf. the
whole encyclical, *Aeterni Patris*, August 4, 1879).

It was on the Feast of St. Dominic in 1880
that Pope Leo XIII, with the unanimous con-
sent of the Sacred Congregation of Rites, for
the glory of God Almighty and honour of the
angelic doctor, for the advancement of learning and the common good of human society,
declared St. Thomas to be the patron of all
Catholic Universities, Colleges, and schools,
and desired him to be, as such, venerated and
honoured.

LETTER IV
The Theologians, Artists, Etc. of the Order

WITH ST. THOMAS, THE FOUNDA-
tions of Dominican theology were laid
for ever. Disciples came to explain his works, to
comment on them, to develop them, to defend
them; few were so foolhardy as to wish to
change them. Ambrose of Siena might arise—a
genius sufficiently powerful to establish his system side by side with St. Thomas's—but with
heroic humility he threw his notes and books
into the fire, out of respect for the Master,
and to preserve unity of teaching in the Order.
Besides, what surer guide could one have, what
more enlightened, than the angelic doctor? It is,
then, no wonder that round him throng numberless commentators, who are great indeed
if they can fully analyse their master's world-
deep thoughts. There is Peter of Tarantaise,
who became the first Dominican Pope under
the name of Innocent V, and has lately been
beatified; Capreolus, whose life-work it was to

defend the teaching of his master; Sylvester of Prierio, who, by command of Leo X, answered the arguments of Luther; Barthelemy de Spina, one of the most learned men of his time, included by Paul III among the five theologians appointed to solve the doubts of the Bishops at the Council of Trent; Melchior Canus,[6] the creator of the modern school of apologetics; Peter Soto, the last Dominican whose voice was heard lecturing publicly in Oxford; Francis Sylvester of Ferrara, surnamed *Ferrariensis*, whose commentary is the standard work on the *Summa contra Gentiles*; more than all, Thomas de Vio, better known as Cardinal Cajetan. Following on his public defence against the famous Pico della Mirandola, he was created Master in Theology at the age of twenty-six.

Nothing of the like had been seen among the Friars Preachers since the days of St. Thomas's triumphs. He was the right hand of Pope Leo X, the most feared of Luther's opponents. He wrote a commentary on the *Summa Theologica* so wonderful that he has since been called the Prince of Commentators, and Leo XIII ordered it to be reprinted with the new Papal edition of St. Thomas's works. Lastly, there are Bañez

---

6 Cardinal Manning said that it was to Canus's book *Loci Theologici* more than any other that he owed his conversion.

and John of St. Thomas—the one celebrated
not merely on account of his connection with
St. Teresa of Ávila, whose spiritual director he
was for eight years, but also for his commen-
taries on the *Summa*, which place him in the
first rank of theologians; the other the glory of
the University of Alcala, and the light of the
Spanish Church of his day. Even in these times,
for those who study his master's works, his
observations will be found always stimulating
and never farfetched.

To scripture and divinity we must add
Canon Law, to make up the complete number of ecclesiastical sciences. It deals with the
Church in her outer life, in her social and vis-
ible existence. Every society must have a head
and a hierarchy, laws and penalties. To know
the various relations between the members and
the head, the privileges and rights belonging
to the different grades of the hierarchy, the
laws which affect the faithful, the penalties
that fall on the guilty—these are the objects of
the science of Canon Law. St. Raymund of Pennafort, the third Master-General of the Order,
co-founder with St. Peter Nolasco of the Order
of Our Lady of Ransom, takes a high place
among the ranks of canonists. He it was who,
by command of Gregory IX, reduced to order
in a single whole all the pontifical decrees of

that Pope's predecessors. In three years he had completed his gigantic task; and his collection was so famous that it is called even now simply *The Decretals*.

There is only space here for just a brief mention of other sciences. The Order[7] can boast of St. Antoninus, Archbishop of Florence, as the creator of what is commonly called moral theology; of Vincent of Beauvais, who resumed in his Speculum Majus all the natural science, philosophy, and history of the thirteenth century; of Melchior Canus, the master of the philosophy of history; of James of Voragine, whose *Golden Legend* is one of the most perfect pieces of Christian poetic imagination. In the arts, the names spring to the mind of Fra Angelico and Fra Bartolomeo, of Fra Sisto and Fra Ristoro, who designed the Bargello and St. Maria Novella in Florence and the Minerva in Rome; of Jerome[8] Savonarola, the master who, without using pencil or brush, himself gave of his genius to others, firing

7 Of the English Province one may mention Nicholas Trivet, the most accurate chronicler of our English Kings; Gregory the Grammarian, or Richard Frauncis, as he is sometimes called, a Norfolk Dominican, who compiled the first English-Latin dictionary; Clement Taylor, the Scot, whose musical pieces contemporaries averred to be the equals of those of Guido of Arezzo.
8 Cf. *Savonarola and the Reformation*, by the Very Rev. J. Procter, O. P., a reply to Dean Farrar, C. T. S.

them no less with his own love of restrained, severe, and manly art.

Tell me an act, name me a science, in which the Dominicans have not one name at least to bespeak their glory.

The sons of St. Dominic have been in truth, as Pope Honorius prophesied, the lights of the world, casting their beams through the darkness and gloom. They have been children of enthusiasm, for they have been also full of a sure and zealous faith—a faith that could but give living force to the hand that wrote or graved or painted the Name of that God Who was the love of all their souls and the source of all their beauty. For what else is beauty than a smile upon the transfigured face of truth?

LETTER V
The Preachers and Missionaries of the Order

A N ORDER OF APOSTLES IS NOT only an Order of teachers; it is even more an Order of preachers and missionaries. The Order of St. Dominic has been in a special way a missionary Order from its very foundation up to our own time. We have seen how preaching is the essential note of Dominican life, the formal object St. Dominic had in view when he founded his Order. To show that the Friars Preachers have lived up to their ideal would be to unroll the long scroll of Dominican history. What famous names would be called up from the past during those seven centuries, from the names of Jordan of Saxony and Reginald of Orleans to the names of Lacordaire and Monsabré.[9]

9 The English Province can boast among its preachers Thomas Waleys, John Bromyard, Robert Holcot, and Nicholas Gorham, who were famed in medieval England. Among the members of the Irish Province of our own day stands out the name of Father Thomas Burke. Cardinal Manning's eulogium of him as one who popularised theology cannot be overmatched.

All this is too well known to need developing but what you have probably heard less about is the zeal of our missionaries in far-distant lands.

St. Dominic himself had very earnestly desired to carry the light of the Gospel to the uncivilized nations. "When we have established," he said to a companion, "we shall go out to evangelize the Cuman Tartars." For this purpose, he let his beard grow, and waited patiently for the first opportunity to set out. But God willed him to be a missionary, not in his own person, but in his children.

In the lifetime of St. Dominic, Paul of Hungary founded a province on the very frontiers of those Cumans, whom our Holy Father had longed to convert. The Dominicans were settled on the boundaries of Servia and Bulgaria amid that horde of peoples, driven by each successive Tartar invasion to the mouth of the Danube. At the same time, St. Hyacinth and Blessed Ceslas, leaving St. Dominic in Rome, strode like giants in the glorious ways of the apostolate. Blessed Ceslas preached the Gospel in Bohemia, Silesia, and Poland; St. Hyacinth pushed on to the very remotest borders of the then known world. He founded, as he went, the Province of Germany and organised that of Poland. In Prussia and Lithuania he helped by his own zeal and that of his brethren the work of civilization begun by the Teutonic Knights. He established the Dominican Provinces of Scandinavia, which had peopled with priories the snow wastes of Greenland two hundred years before America was discovered. St. Hyacinth went through White Russia and Red Russia, breasted the Tartar Invasions, reaching by the Black Sea the Grecian Archipelago; thence, turning towards Central Asia, he penetrated into Tibet and China (then known as "far Cathay"). On every side he left traces of his zeal, sowing miracles along his way, converting heretics and heathens.

Almost simultaneously St. Raymund of Pennafort was directing the zeal of his brethren along the barbaric coasts of Africa and founding convents up to Tunis and Tripoli.

The Order of St. Dominic, then, with a rapidity that appears quite miraculous, took from its beginning the most advanced outposts of Christianity, from whence it might push out into those tribes that knew not Christ.[10] Such

10 Many brethren from the British Isles joined in this holy crusade. Three from England went to convert the Saracens in 1321. Henry of England was Archbishop in Russia in 1244, and converted the King of Litten in Livonia. About 1248, Father Thomas from England was Bishop of Ebron in Palestine; Father William was Archbishop of Rages (his tombstone can still be seen at Rhyddlan in Flintshire); Father Richard was Bishop in Lesser Tartary in 1330; Father Bennet went from Scotland to fill the see of Panido in Romania in 1468.

were the members, such the zeal of these missionaries, that they spread by thousands among
the savages and pagans. Thus in 1253—that
is to say, thirty-two years after the death of
St. Dominic—Innocent IV, writing to the Friars Preachers, addressed his letter to them in
these terms: "To our dearly-beloved sons, the
Friars Preachers, preaching in the lands of
the Saracens, Greeks, Bulgars, Cumans, Ethi-
opians, Syrians, Goths, Jacobites, Armenians,
Indians, Tartars, Hungarians, and other hea-
then peoples of the East, health and apostolic
benediction," etc. Nothing had been seen like
it since the days of the Apostles. The work of
the Dominicans in the East is without par-
allel in all history, save for the work of the
Franciscans at the very same time. The children of St. Francis and St. Dominic, inflamed
with the same true zeal, halved between them
the continent of Asia. To the Friars Minor the
Pope gave the metropolitan see of Kaubaluk
(Pekin), to the Friars Preachers that of Solta-
nieh. But this division did not prevent a certain overlapping of territories. In 1291 a son
of St. Francis received the last breath of a
son of St. Dominic at St. Thomeus of Melia-
pore, while a son of St. Dominic administered
the Sacraments of the Dying to a son of St.
Francis at Pekin. Nor was it long before the

whole coat of Africa had heard the voice of a Friar Preacher—Guinea, the Congo, the Cape of Good Hope, Mozambique, and Nubia—these religious went everywhere, following, accompanying, even at Tunis preceding the boldest explorer, everywhere preaching the glad tidings of the new Gospel, and making Christ Our Lord honoured and loved.

Again, it was owing to the support of Diego of Deza and some other Dominicans at the Junta of Salamanca that Christopher Columbus triumphed at last over the critics of his day. He went out, supported on land by the Dominicans in the councils of Kings, supported at sea by the Franciscans amid the mutiny of his men and the turbulence of the waves. No sooner had he discovered America, and the Spanish galleons sailed for the New World, than at once there spread among the Dominicans a zeal and a passion to embark and carry the name of Christ to shores that knew it not. They went out to evangelise these heathens. Among them shone St. Lewis Bertrand, the apostle of Cartagena and the neighbouring countries, who converted and baptised thousands of the poor natives.

The Dominicans were the apostles of these wild tribes; they were no less their defenders. Who can mention without a thrill of emotion the name of Bartholomew de las Casas, who braved so well the obloquy of his fellow-Spaniards and the terrors of the ocean, which he crossed seven times to defend the cause of the poor Indians?[11]

So intense was the zeal for these far-off missions displayed by the Order of St. Dominic that a special congregation was founded for those who desired to consecrate themselves to this work.

11 "The present day is a witness to the missionary spirit of the Order. In Africa the Sisters have foundations spread through Mashonaland, Bastuoland, Zululand, the Transvaal, and Cape Colony; they are formed into one congregation recruited from Germany and Ireland and attend to the instruction of the natives. Trinidad and Grenada are the missions of the Irish and English fathers. The leper settlement of Cocorite is attended to by the French Sisters. The Mossul mission, comprising Mesopotamia and Kurdistan, belongs to the French. The Archbishops of these missions are taken from the Order, while the religious have their schools, colleges, printing-presses, and parishes to attend to. The Dutch have their West India Isles. The Spaniards, French, and Belgians scattered over Brazil and Chile are endeavouring to reclaim the savages of Ecuador. The missionary Province of the Philippines, under the care of the Spaniards, had, in 1896, over 600 members, with eleven Bishops of the Order, charged with the care of beyond 900,000 Catholics and training the native clergy for five vicarates in China and Tonquin. The Dominion of Canada is one of the most flourishing centres of Dominican enterprise. St. Joseph's Province (now including the mission in Cuba and the Philippines), in the United States, is in the forefront both in point of numbers and undertakings. California, lately raised to a Province, completes the field of North American missionary zeal. Australia and New Zealand in southern latitudes have their own pioneer missionaries from the British Isles." (*Dominican Order*, by Father Placid Conway, O. P., Scottish C. T. S., 17–19)

They were called "the travellers for the Name of Jesus Christ." The congregation fulfilled so well the hopes of the Pope, and procured for the Church so large a number of missionaries and martyrs, that the Sovereign Pontiff, in memory of the blood shed by the first heroes of this band, gave its members the right of wearing (as do the Cardinals) scarlet girdles, shoes, and skull-caps. We have mentioned martyrs! How long, how monotonous almost, is the unending list of the Dominican martyrology! Its pages are written on every shore of the world. Let us turn these records over together.

LETTER VI
The Martyrs of the Order

IN THE DAYS OF ST. DOMINIC, THE Province of Hungary produced its legions of Dominican martyrs. In a single massacre there were two hundred holocausts to truth—that is, two hundred witnesses for the faith that was in them. Later, Blessed Paul, after having converted many infidels to the Church of Christ, poured out his own life-blood in 1242, along with ninety of his brethren, some of whom were burnt alive, others beheaded, others shot with arrows, others pierced with spears. In 1260 Blessed Sadoc was martyred at Sandomir with forty-seven of his brethren. The story goes that on the eve of their death the brother who was reading out of the martyrology in choir found written there in letters of gold; "At Sandomir, the passion of forty-eight martyrs." They were slaughtered by the Tartars as they chanted in choir the *Salve Regina*. The very next year, 1261, two hundred Friars Preachers, who were evangelising Damietta, were slain by the sword of the Mussulman. But who can number the myriads of the Order of St. Dominic that went to receive the crown of martyrdom in the East Indies, in North and South America, as well as on the coasts of Africa, on the banks of the Ganges, amid the inhospitable lands of China, Indochina, and Japan? Take one single instance, that tells its tale with an eloquence without compare. It was in 1355 that Benedict XII, a monk of Citeaux, yielding to the ideas of certain persons, who thought the life of the Friars Preachers to be too severe, spoke of modifying the Rule and Constitutions. Men said that such severity was incompatible with a vigorous apostolate. To reply to this objection, drawn from merely human wisdom, the General Chapter of the Order sitting at Valencia ordered a list of the Dominican Martyrs between 1234 and 1335 to be drawn up.

The total given was no less than 13,370. That was the only reply made by the Friars Preachers.[12] The total had risen to 26,000 in the sixteenth century.

In the seventeenth century Japan brings also her list of martyrs. Along with Blessed Alphonsus de Navarette, 205 died for their faith, of

---

12 Of course, the round numbers and statistics of the Middle Ages, as of every age, must not be taken too exactly.

whom more than half belonged to the Order
of St. Dominic. Benedict XIV said that their
"cause," when introduced at Rome, was the
most interesting of its time. The desire of these
men for martyrdom was astonishing. Blessed
Alphonsus, in a transport of Divine delight,
wrote, in the midst of his torments: "O my
God, this is too much—not of suffering but of
consolation in suffering."

Among the greatest martyrs of Japan were
William Courtet and Michel Orazata, who said
amid their pains: "O Jesus, it is sweet to suffer for Thee; Queen of the most holy Rosary,
pray for us." The executioners drove pins
under their nails, and then drew one hand
over the other, as though they were musical
instruments. The martyrs knew naught else
to say than this: "Oh, what sweet harmony,
that heralds us into Paradise!" And one, see-
ing the drops of blood oozing from his fingers,
cried out in ecstasy: "What beautiful rubies
drip from my fingers! What crimson roses! It
is my blood that tints them—my blood shed
for Thee, O Jesus!" Nor has it been among
savage races only that the list of martyrs has
grown great. In North Italy, for example, St.
Peter of Verona, struck by a heretic's dagger,
as he lay dying, wrote on the ground with
the blood that flowed from his wounds, *Credo*

in unum Deum. He was raised to the altars of the Church. After him, in the same joyous triumph, followed Antony Pavaonio, Antiby Neyrot, Peter of Ruffia, Bartholomew of Savilianni. Then, in the South of France, were the martyrs of Avignonette. St. John of Gorcum made holy the soil of Holland by giving his life in defence of the primacy of the Pope and the dogma of the Real Presence.[13] In England, Ireland, and Scotland, a glorious band suffered as the victims of Protestantism. Take the story of Father Barry, Dominican Prior of Cashel, in Ireland. The captain of the band charged with his execution was so struck with his noble and holy appearance that he offered him his life if he would only fling off his habit. But the Prior, with heroic contempt, replied: "This habit is for me the livery of Christ and an emblem

13 In England, of the First Order suffered Blessed Robert Nutter and others, and of the Third Order Blessed Adrian Fortescue; in Scotland F. George Criton, F. John Black, etc.; in Ireland, says the General Chapter held at Rome in 1656, "Abundant was the harvest that in our own times ripened there for the heavenly Master of those, forsooth, who suffered extreme torture for the Catholic faith. Of forty-three convents that our Order possessed in that island, not one remains; all, through the fury of the heretics, have been consumed by fire, razed to the ground, or devoted to profane purposes. In the year 1646, we numbered 600 friars; now not 150 remain, and even these are exiles from their native land, the rest being either crowned with martyrdom or condemned to a lingering death on the Island of Barbadoes."

of His Passion; it is the banner of the military service I owe Him. Since my youth have I worn it; I will not now give it up in my old age." Then they seized him, placed a fire under him, and finally cut off the head that their threats could not bend.

For fear of being wearisome, we will end now by mentioning those who fell in Tonquin in the last century. We can give, of course, the names of the leaders only: Bishop Ignatius Delgado,[14] who died for his faith in prison, July 21, 1838; Bishop Dominic Henares, his coadjutor, beheaded July 25, 1838; Father Joseph Fernandez, Vicar-Provincial, beheaded July 24, 1838; Bishop Joseph Mary Diaz, beheaded July 20, 1857; Bishop Melchior Garcia san Pedro, cut in pieces on July 28, 1858; Bishop Jerome[15] Hermonsillas and Bishop Valentine Berio-Ochoa, both beheaded November 1, 1861, one of them—Bishop Melchior—repeating each time that the axe cut off one of his limbs or the knife a piece of his flesh, *Deo gratias, Deo gratias.*

Does this not show how unfailingly God demands witnesses to His Name from the

14 Blessed Ignatius, Dominic, etc., beatified by Leo XIII in 1900.
15 Blessed Jerome, Valentine, etc., beatified by Pius X in 1906.

Order of St. Dominic, and how unfailingly the Order answers His demand, by producing, not merely men eloquent in their speech, but also men who preach by their blood?

LETTER VII
The Rule: Study, Prayer, Monastic Observances

WE HAVE SEEN, THEREFORE, that the Order has truly realised the intentions of St. Dominic. It now remains merely to explain the means by which it has done so. To produce and fashion these religious so great before God and man, these unnumbered legions of Saints, apostles, teachers, missionaries, and martyrs, what means did the Order make us of? The same that St. Dominic had laid down—viz., study and contemplation, joined to the monastic life and observance, to the choral office by day and night.

From the beginning the Dominican priories were true homes of study and learning. St. Dominic knew that if all success comes from God, God nevertheless demands from us all our efforts to attain it. Hence he sent his first disciples to the Universities to follow the lectures on philosophy and theology. Hence he unceasingly bade them devote themselves to the study of the sacred sciences. The Friars Preachers thenceforward organized in their priories those courses of study which produced such marvelous results. The monastic observances were to lose nothing of their austerity, prayer and the Divine Office nothing of their splendour and regularity, but yet the Rule was to be adapted to all circumstances so as to encourage study. It was only after prolonged years of preparation that the new religious were allowed to preach, or even to go abroad on the foreign missions. Thus formed, they could accomplish the words of St. Paul: "Preach the Word; be instant in season, out of season; reprove, entreat, rebuke in all patience and doctrine" (2 Tim. 4:2). So well did the Friars Preachers follow out the counsels of their holy founder, so abundantly did God bless their earnest efforts, that they surpassed their masters in Divine learning. From the days of Blessed Albert and St. Thomas Aquinas, it was no longer they who sought the Universities, but the Universities—even the most famous in Europe—that sought them for their most brilliant professors. About the year 1320, the Sovereign Pontiff gave their schools the same privileges as Universities—that is to say, the right of teaching philosophy and theology in public, and of conferring the title of "Doctor." The Order remained ever faithful to

this great tradition of its founder.[16] ever has
it ceased to urge on its members the study of
the higher sciences. Each Master-General, each
General Chapter, has done its best to foster,
encourage, and develop the existing schools of
the day. Nor has it been merely the young nov-
ices who have been urged to study; the other
Fathers, who have grown grey in the labours of
the apostolate, are continually having it borne
in upon them that no true son of St. Dominic can ever arrive at any age when he may
lay aside his books and cease to apply himself
to his priestly studies. So this zeal for knowledge has become a hall-mark of a Dominican
vocation. The student of history knows that all
the Saints of our Order have been recognised
in their own day as masters, and that their
labours availed not only for their contemporaries, but also for their posterity.

Of course, the love and study of St. Thomas's
works have always been strong in the Order.

16 Oxford produced some 300 Doctors, beginning with
Robert Bacon and Richard Fitzacre in St. Edward's Schools.
At a later period the Friars Preachers entered Cambridge,
were the co-founders of Dublin and Glasgow, and took an
active part in Aberdeen and St. Andrews. The American
Province has built quite recently a large college for Dominican students at the new Catholic University at Washington,
where, indeed, the Dominicans hold at least one chair of
theology. At Freibury (Suisese) nearly twenty Dominicans
of many nationalities are among the Professors. Time alone
can show what will be the relation between the Irish Province and the National Universities.

Take this one modern example out of many. Bishop Valentine Ochoa, martyred in Tonquin in 1861, proposed towards the end of his life to learn by heart the whole of the *Summa* of the Angelic Doctor. Every day he studied two articles, and this amid the duties of his charge and the nameless horrors of a terrible persecution.

We must study, St. Thomas would say, as though we counted on ourselves only to acquire learning; we must pray as if we counted only on our prayers and sacrifices to obtain it. Faithful to this counsel and to the example of St. Thomas himself (as he also was faithful to that of St. Dominic), the Dominicans always made study to keep even pace with the monastic observances. So far from finding these austerities a bar to the progress of learning, they realized them to be the greatest helps in their work. They knew that the deeper the soul was steeped in the purifying practises of penance, the nearer did it approach to God; and that the nearer it drew to God, the more it entered into all light. They knew that souls were more easily purchased and made free by prayer and sacrifice than by word of mouth or personal effort. The most learned Dominicans have been the most constant in their religious observances. Witness St. Thomas, St. Raymund, St. Vincent Ferrer, St. Pius V, and others. The most zealous in their studies, they have been also the most austere, the most faithful to their Rule, the first in choir by day and night for the public recitation of the Divine Office. The last has always been considered as one of the essentials of the life of the Order. The children of St. Dominic have never forgotten it. To fulfil in the name of the Church the great duty of public prayer is for them an honour of which they are justly proud. To render to God this official praise of the people amid their brethren, at the foot of the tabernacle, in the company of Angels and Saints, appeared to them as the sweetest rest in the midst of the hundred fatigues of the apostolate and the austerities of the Rule.

Study, the monastic observances, the solemn recitation of the Divine Office—such, then, are the means the Order has always made use of for the formation of apostles after St. Dominic's own heart. Not one of these means has ever prevented the efficient working of the other two. Quite the reverse. The centuries and the countries when and where the Order flourished most have been precisely those in which the monastic life, study, and the liturgy have been observed with the greater zeal and the more minute accuracy.

LETTER VIII
The Order and
Modern Times

THERE ARE, OF COURSE, SOME objections which will suggest themselves to you. The fact that the Order answered so fully to the ideas of St. Dominic and the needs of the Church in the past does not prevent the further question from being asked: Does it meet equally efficiently the needs of modern times? In other words, does its formal object in any way affect the religious needs of today? Even if the end for which the Order was instituted is still of equal value, what shall we say of the means employed? Surely they do not harmonize with our new manner of living and our increasing physical weakness? Is not the Rule a great deal too severe? Does it not overtax the nervous, unbalanced state of the men of our time?

These are, I venture to think, two obvious objections. To the first, I reply that the Order of St. Dominic has in the past merited the

name of the Order of Truth—that its destiny
is to spread the truth, to defend and avenge
it by its teachers and preachers, its martyrs
and missionaries. If, then, its whole organization is built up especially for this object, who
can venture to suggest that such an Order as
this is not as needful in every age as is truth
itself? For God has made the Friars Preachers the champions of truth. And, assuredly, if
there was ever a time in the history of the
world when truth had need of a champion, it
is in these days of ours, when it is held in
such contempt and outraged in so many ways;
when in the pages of numberless books and on
the lips of the sensualist, the philosopher, and
the historian are repeated the sneering words
of Pilate: "What is truth?" Now, to avenge the
rights and honour of truth, its champion has
need of arms and armour fitted for the fight he
must wage. The arms and armour of the Dominican Order—that time-honoured champion in
every tourney against error—have they become
rusty? Pope Leo XIII emphatically answered,
"No!" when he bade his children apply to St.
Thomas for weapons against modern attacks
on our beliefs. For it is St. Thomas who is the
treasury of the Preaching Friars, the arsenal
from which they choose their arms for the con-
quest of every error, schism, and heresy.

To possess such powerful weapons of defence is one thing; to know how to use them is another.

It is good to have the right books, but it is a great deal better to be able to explain and expound and interpret them in the right way. Now, it stands to reason that the children of St. Dominic, the brethren of St. Thomas, are the authentic exponents of their master's teaching—that the long tradition handed down by living teachers in an unbroken succession, the same all the world over, is likely to be the truest test of an accurate exposition. Moreover, the guarantee of this fidelity has been that every Dominican professor must first have taken his degree, whether as Lector,[17] Bachelor, or Master, in St. Thomas's own works. These titles can be obtained only after long years of study. For the Lectorate the course is seven years, and this degree suffices for being nominated Professor. After seven further years of actual teaching comes an examination for the Bachelorship, and finally, after a second spell of seven years' teaching, the supreme degree of the Mastership. It is all this that has made the Supreme Pontiffs, as century after century

---

17   The title of Lector in Sacred Theology is the old equivalent for the modern Doctor of Divinity.

rolled by, recognise the Friars Preachers as the
official exponents of the doctrine of their master and brother, Thomas of Aquino.

But, even granting that the end for which
the Order was founded and its learning still
hold good, a critic may, of course, suggest
that, all the same, the medieval monastic
observances, the long fasts, the perpetual fish
diet, and the public recitation of the Divine
Office, may nevertheless prevent the very real-
ization of that purpose which is no doubt so
excellent.

To the second objection, therefore, I reply
that it is hardly a Christian one. If the world
is dying of starvation from want of truth, it
is dying no less from excess of pleasure and
indulgence. If in every age the preacher of the
Gospel must react against sensual softness by
upholding the ideal of austerity, and against
an immoderate desire for wealth by the ideal
of voluntary poverty, surely such doctrine was
never so needed as today. If in every age an
apostle can only be a true apostle on the condition of uniting to the Blood of Our Lord Jesus
Christ shed for men's souls, his own unwea-
ried labours, his own austerities, penances, and
self-sacrifice, surely a modern apostle can be
no exception to such a rule. If in every age
prayer—and, above all, public prayer—has

been the gentle, kindly dew that gives life and increase to the studies and sermons of the preacher, surely it is still so today. These things are in truth so essential that an Order of Preachers cannot afford to lay them aside. Nay, more: we say in all seriousness that if this Order, founded for so noble an object, and making use of such powerful means, existed no longer, it would be necessary to resuscitate it. But, you will say, is the life of mortification and self-sacrifice that in theory is so beautiful an ideal really and truly practical? Are we, men of these modern days of rush and hurry—are we capable of the long fasts, fish diet, and midnight Office? Would it not be as swell to modify the Rule a little, so as to allow more men to enter it and help it to its purpose?[18]

Dear friend, for six centuries this same objection has been made in exactly the same words as you have put it today, and six centuries of experience echo exactly the same reply. It is this: the ages most fruitful, vigorous, and glorious that our Order can boast in history

18 It may be noted that in the three English-speaking Provinces, owing to the rudeness of the climate and stress of work, the midnight Office is anticipated or else postponed, so that the sleep remains unbroken. Matins and Lauds are either about 9 p.m. or 4 a.m., according to local custom or the season of the year.

were precisely those in which the children of St. Dominic have found their strength and energy in a life of penance and stern austerity, as Samuel the prophet and Samson, God's athlete, found theirs in fasting and in the frugal bread of the poor.

That is the answer of history. Should you desire the answer of science too, here it is: The most competent physicians of today tell us that our modern weakness comes from our over-indulgence, that the ruin of our health comes from excess and undue refinement in the matter of food. Many even of our most respected medical men assure us that in very many ways a vegetable diet is best. Not, of course, that the monastic life is easy for human nature, but that it is not so difficult as we are probably apt to think it, and that it is by no means beyond our strength.[19]

The question, then, of the strictness and austerity of the Rule is not really a serious obstacle to the vocation of a young man who feels drawn to devote himself to God's glory and to the salvation of souls in the Order

19   The diet is tempered in the English, Irish, and American Provinces by the use of meat at the midday meal at least three times a week—viz., on Sundays, Tuesdays, and Thursdays. In case of need, Superiors not only may, but must, modify the austerities by dispensation. Legitimate dispensation is an essential element in the Dominican Rule.

of St. Dominic. Once more, to live up to the Dominican constitutions, all that is required is ordinary health. Rather, what has been lacking during six centuries, and is still lacking today, is not health, but that which bends all things and is never itself bent—that which God's grace even can never force or compel—the power of human will.

LETTER IX
Entrance Into the Order

THIS LETTER IS MERELY TO explain to you how to join the Order of St. Dominic and to give you the more important details regarding the novitiate and the studies.

No one can be admitted until after his sixteenth birthday, nor until he has completed his classical studies. On joining, the candidate must present testimonial letters from the Bishop of his diocese, and, in fact, from the Bishops of all the dioceses in which he has lived after his fifteenth year. These letters are to certify to his age, knowledge, and conduct. Further, he must not be in debt, nor be necessary for the support of his family, nor have worn the habit of any other religious Order or Congregation (without a dispensation from the Master-General), nor have made profession in any other Order or Congregation (without Papal Dispensation). The Order cannot accept any sum of money from any novice until he has taken his vows, except the necessary expenses of his keep, if these are spontaneously offered. He lives during this time on the fruits of the labours of other members of the community, and on the alms generously given by benefactors to desire to take part in the merits of the apostolate. A special organisation under the direction of the Provincial Procurator is established to enable the Fathers to carry on the expensive work of the candidate's novitiate and studentship.

When a young man determines to join the novitiate, he should write to the Very Rev. Father Provincial.[20] If he is accepted on trial, he then goes to the novitiate house, where he must pass an examination in Latin, etc. After that comes a retreat of ten days, at the end of which he receives the black-and-white habit of St. Dominic, taking a new name, and begins at once his simple novitiate. This lasts for twelve months at least and eighteen at most, and is spent exclusively studying his vocation and in forming the new religious according to the Dominican spirit. He applies himself to learning the constitutions and rubrics, assists at the choral Office and at the little Office of Our Lady, exercises his mind and heart

20   In England, St. Dominic's Priory, Haverstock Hill, London, N.W; in Ireland, St. Saviour's Priory, Dorset Street, Dublin; in America, Convent of St. Dominic, Washington.

in contemplation and meditation, takes part
in the reading of the Lives of the Saints and
other spiritual books—in a word, is present
at all exercises of the community. At the end
of that year he takes simple (but perpetual)
vows of poverty, chastity, and obedience, which
are dispended by the Holy See only for very
grave reasons. Once he has taken his vows, the
young religious enters on his professed novitiate, and three years later he is allowed to
make his solemn profession. In another year
or two, according to his age, he receives Holy
Orders, and eventually the priesthood. Then
he leaves the novitiate, though continuing to
study theology, before he is allowed to engage
in the great ministry of preaching. The studies
commence immediately after simple profession.
Three years are given to philosophy and four
to theology.

Provided a man has the requisite conditions,
he can join the Order at any age. Of course,
the priesthood is no obstacle to entering. Many
of our Saints became Dominicans late in life,
and after years of useful ministry. Priests take
their simple and solemn vows like the others,
but the Master-General often allows them a
shorter course of studies.

And now, what remains still unsaid? I have
explained to you the object of the Order; I

have told you some of its glorious history; I have endeavoured to show you the want that it came to fill. Have I put it in such a way as to attract you to love it? I know not. The only thing I know: that, judging from my own personal experience of the sweetness and consolations of this life, I dare to repeat to you the words of St. Paul to Agrippa (Acts 26:28, 29): "And Agrippa said to Paul, In a little thou persuadest me to be a Christian. And Paul said, I would to God that both in a little and in much, not only thou, but also all that hear me this day, should become such as I also am." But I, looking at the pleasant chains of religious life that hold me captive to Christ and to His Church, lift them up and say, "even with these bands."

It is this sweet constraint that I wish for you in God's Name.

LETTER X
The Devotions
of the Order

THE LIFE OF THE FRIAR Preacher does, then, appeal to you. You appreciate its genius and its beauty. You see how needful it is to the Church, especially in modern times. You have heard the voice of God saying to you, as the Prince of Apostles said to St. Dominic: "Go thou and preach, for unto this art thou called." You have decided to be a Dominican. It is only a question of time as to when you can come to us.

You cannot have arrived at this decision without a certain struggle. Perhaps your friends had bade you stay with them, and had told you that you could save your soul equally well by remaining where you were. But your generous nature has triumphed over that argument. Perhaps your father and mother have asked you not to leave them, because they have loved you so much. Indeed, it is hard to go away from your home and family.[21] Yet it is the voice of God that is calling to you and bidding you love Him even more than you love them. Perhaps it has been urged upon you that, if you want to be a priest, you can be at least a secular priest. Surely, your friends have said to you, the priesthood does not necessarily imply the religious life. You can have one without the other. But you have thought of the young man in the Gospels whom Our Lord looked upon and loved, and to whom He said: "If thou wouldst be perfect, go sell all thou hast, and come and follow Me." Yes, it is the same Master Who has whispered these words to your heart: "Do not remain where you are, in the hope of using your money for My Name's sake. That calling is not for you; but go, sell all thou hast, and then come and follow Me." Yet some time must pass before you can go to the noviciate. What should you do meanwhile? I can think of nothing better to say than this: Learn to love the chief Dominican Devotions.

First and foremost is devotion to the most Holy Sacrament. God has willed that the Order of St. Dominic should have a great

21 Savonarola wrote to his father, after having run away from home to become a Dominican: "Never since I was born did I suffer so great mental anguish as when I felt I was going to leave my own flesh and blood, and go among people who were strangers to me."

share in extending this devotion. St. Dominic taught it to his children as he had learnt it in the long night-watches at the foot of the tabernacle and in the ecstatic moments of his daily Mass. It was our first Dominican Cardinal—Hugh of St. Cher—who, as we have said, undertook the defence of Blessed Juliana and, acting on her inspiration, inaugurated at Liége, with befitting splendour, the first Feast of Corpus Christi. He decreed also that this solemnity should be observed annually in every diocese over which he ruled as Papal Legate. It was owing to the petitions of St. Thomas Aquinas, seconding the efforts of Blessed Juliana, that Pope Urban IV extended this feast to the Universal Church, and it was to him that the Sovereign Pontiff entrusted the task of composing the Office of Corpus Christi. It is this same Office that is chanted on that festival, as well in the great basilica of St. Peter's at Rome as in the backwoods of America, even now after the passing of six hundred years. And a wonderful piece of literature it is. The true doctrine of the Real Presence is expounded in perfect order, with absolute precision and admirable restraint. Every word is full of meaning, has its proper position in the rising or falling cadence, and composes with the rest the rhythmic beat of a perfect poem.

It is full of piety and supernatural love. Who that hears *Lauda Sion* and *Pange Lingua* cannot but feel thrilled as though in the very presence of God? It is perfectly human, yet wonderfully Divine. It is the triumphant paean of the God-Man.

Again, it was Father Dominic Stella who established in the Minerva at Rome the first Confraternity of the Blessed Sacrament. And what shall I say of Blessed Imelda, the little Dominican maid, dying of love in thanksgiving after her first Communion? Or of the beautiful legend of two little boys who, receiving from Blessed Bernard de Morlais the Body of their Lord for the first time, passed away on the altar-steps to the full vision of Him in eternity? Or of St. John of Gorcum, who gave his life in witness to the dogma of the Real Presence? Go often to this heavenly banquet; here you will find gathered together all the Dominican Saints in Heaven and on earth.

Another devotion very dear to the Order is to the Holy Name of Jesus.

In 1274 Blessed Gregory X commanded the Dominicans officially to propagate this devotion. It had been a favourite practise of St. Dominic in his journeyings to chant the hymn to the Holy Name: "Jesu nostra redemption Amor et disderium," etc.

And it was in the power of this blest Name that he had restored life to the nephew of Cardinal Stephen. Naturally, then, the Confraternity of the Holy Name has remained attached to the Order. Repeat often the Name of Jesus.

Use it now as a hymn and a prayer; one day you will preach it.

Devotion to the Sacred Heart has also been popular in the Order since the day when St. Catherine of Siena in vision exchanged her heart with her Loved One's Divine Heart. Remember, too, that the French national vow of a basilica dedicated to the Sacred Heart was first suggested in the Dominican Convent of Poitiers and that the idea was submitted to the approval of Pius IX by the then Master-General of the Order, Pére Jandel.

Further, there is the devotion to the holy purity through the intercession of St. Thomas Aquinas. To it St. Aloysius ascribed his own love of that Christ-like virtue.

Lastly, who dare hope to recount the many claims that link the Order of St. Dominic to the Mother of God?

Legend tells us that it was she who asked of her Divine Son that the Order might be founded; who gave with her own hands to Blessed Reginald the white Dominican scapular, who showed herself in vision to St. Dominic, going from bed to bed of the brethren as they slept, smiling to them and blessing them, as a mother would smile on and bless her own children. To Blessed Jordan she revealed herself: "I am that Holy Queen about whom thou and thine chant evening by evening in the *Salve Regina*, and at the words, 'Turn, then, O most gracious Advocate,' I prostate myself at the feet of my Son to demand His blessing on thy Order." And St. Dominic saw her children nestling beneath the folds of her imperial mantle amid the splendour of the stars.

Last of all, she taught him the Rosary, the sweetest and most beautiful tribute we can pay her. It is her favourite devotion, the easiest and yet the most profound; the most popular and yet the most theological; the most enriched of all with indulgences. Leo XIII, like all his predecessors, proclaimed St. Dominic to be its institutor and so confided to his children, and to his children alone, the care of the Rosary Confraternity in every part of the globe. And when in times past this devotion had fallen out of use, amid the clash of arms and the distress of terrible wars, Mary herself appeared to Alan de la Roche to repeat to him what she had said to his Father: "Go thou and preach my Rosary, that men may be saved." It is indeed a Dominican devotion. Through it, at the prayers of St. Pius V, Mary gained form her Son the miraculous deliverance of Christendom on the waters of Lepanto.[22] Take, then, this Rosary, love and use it until the day when you shall also preach it.

Now I must make an end. I shall do so by telling you what I have found in a quaint old chronicler. "We Dominicans," says he, with pleasing pride, "are so truly Our Lady St. Mary's Order, that alone, as I well believe, of all religious, we make our vow of obedience into her hands."

This is indeed how our vow runs, that dates back to the age of chivalry: "I make profession and vow obedience to God, to Blessed Mary, ever a Virgin, to St. Dominic, and to you, Master-General of the Friars Preachers, according to the Rule of the Blessed Augustine and the Constitutions of the Order of Friars Preachers, that I will be obedient to you and your successors until death." Is not this beautifully worded? He who, under the

22 Thirty years after Queen Elizabeth had set up Protestantism, rosaries were still openly used in Wales. The common people said that they could read upon their beads and others did upon their books, and made such "clappings" with them in the church that it was complained the minister could hardly be heard for the noise. Confraternities of the Rosary flourished through all the times of persecution and aided in secret the heroic courage of our fathers.

inspiration of God and the blessing of God's Mother, has solemnly sworn to it can desire no greater happiness here below. He has plighted his troth to God, to Our Lady, so St. Dominic *usque ad mortem*—until death unites him to them aided in secret the heroic courage of our fathers.

APPENDIX I
The Lay Brothers

THIS NAME IS GIVEN TO THOSE religious who have done no studies, and who cannot, therefore, aspire to the priesthood. They are mainly occupied with the manual labour of the Priory. Like the priests, they observe the perpetual fish diet, the long fast from September 14 till Easter, and take the triple vow of poverty, chastity, and obedience. They are real religious and participate in the privileges and indulgences of the Order, just as they keep its rule and austerities. Are, then, these Brothers outside the scope of the Order because they can neither study not nor preach, nor work for the salvation of souls in the same way as the Fathers do? Not at all. Far from being foreign to the purpose of the Order, they are indispensable to its proper working. The Fathers could not, without grave inconvenience, spend their time in preparing the meals, sweeping the cloisters, mending and washing the clothes, and so forth. Without these lay

Brothers, then, there would have to be servants in the house, which would be extremely awkward for obvious reasons, and, according to the Constitutions, "a source of much evil." The Brothers, then, do not preach; they study only what is sufficient for their work, and for the sanctification of their souls. Yet, by their humble labour they are an inestimable boon to a religious Order, and make it possible for the Fathers to study and preach. They have a part, therefore, in the good works of the priests, in their merits before God, and consequently in their reward. Besides this, cannot the Brothers offer to God the trying occupations of each day, the penances and fasts, the prayers and thousand acts of self-sacrifice that come necessarily into religious life? Surely they can. And so, without preaching or study, they yet become in very truth Friars Preachers.

Indeed, those are true Friars Preachers who so effectively help continue the great work of St. Dominic as do these lay Brothers, so of whom, like Blessed Martin Porres and Blessed John Messias, were favoured with God's highest gifts and graces, and were illuminated with a Divine wisdom that astonished in its fullness the greatest theologians. Indeed, those are true Preaching Brothers, those numberless lay Brothers who have accompanied our missionaries into far-off lands, helping them to preach the Gospel to heathens, to instruct the children, to organize the convert Christians, to witness with them to the truths of faith by their blood in a martyr's death. Yes, assuredly they rightly bear on earth the proud name of Friars Preachers, and they will receive in Heaven the reward of the Preaching Brotherhood.[23]

23 "Lay-postulants cannot be admitted to the habit until they have completed their twentieth year. In the English Province, however, we are allowed to receive them when they have completed their eighteenth year." (*A Manual for Dominican Lay Brothers*, by F. Hugh Pope. This booklet explains the life and spirit of the Dominican lay brothers.)

APPENDIX II
The Second and Third Orders of St. Dominic, for Women Living in Community

WE HAVE SEEN IN THE FOREGO-ing letters how the sons of St. Dominic have succeeded in carrying out the design of their Founder in the true idea of the Dominican spirit—viz., "the union of action and contemplation, the blending of the two to the prejudice of neither, the working together of the active and contemplative spirits," in order to the attainment of one end—the salvation of souls.

But St. Dominic had spiritual daughters as well as sons, and a short sketch of their life and work in the economy of the Order my not unfitly find a place in these pages.

The Order of St. Dominic has a triple organization, which opens a large field for this apostolate. The "Great," or First Order, as we have seen, comprises the Fathers, students, and lay Brothers. This foundation, however, was not the first in order of time. In the year 1206, when the future Founder was known only as "Brother Dominic, the preacher against the heretics," he gathered together, as the first-fruits of his apostolate, so Blessed Jordan tells us, "certain noble women," who had been delivered over to the heretics by their relations, to be trained and corrupted by the latter's abominable teaching. St. Dominic converted a number of these ladies, and formed them into a religious community. Some writers are of opinion that his chief intention in founding this first convent of Our Lady at Prouille was to make it a house of education for young girls. Pére Danzas strongly combats this view, and maintains that, whilst preserving the daughters of the Catholics from the hands of the sectaries, who had already found them powerful instruments in the propagation of their heresy, the Holy Father's principal design was to associate the religious of Prouille with the great work that was ripening in his mind, but which had not yet blossomed into life.

"Prayer," says Pére Danzas, "is the source of action; contemplation that of the apostolate." And so for ten years these eldest children of

the Dominican family laboured by their prayers
and penances for the birth of that glorious
Order of which their great patriarch was to
be the Father. Before his death, St. Dominic founded three more monasteries (as they
were then called) of cloistered women, those of
Madrid and of Gormas in Spain and St. Sixtus
in Rome. A fifth, the Convent of St. Agnes, in
Bologna, was left unfinished by the Holy Father,
but it was completed by his successor, Blessed
Jordan of Saxony, in conjunction with his holy
penitent, Diana d'Andalo, who, together with
the Sisters Cecilia and Amata, of the same convent, is now raised to the altars of the Church
and ranks among many beatified members of
the Order.

The communities of the Second Order spread
rapidly throughout Europe. At the beginning
of the fourteenth century a list of forty-nine
convents is given by Bernard Guidonis. Their
number has gone on increasing, even up to
the present day, in spite of persecutions and
dispersions.

There is one convent of Dominican nuns of
the Second Order in England. This community, English from the beginning, was founded
in 1661 by the Dominican Cardinal Howard
at Valvorde, in Belgium. The first to take the
habit was his cousin, Sister Antonia Howard.

She was professed on her death-bed a few
months afterwards, "consoled by a vision of
Our Lady of the Rosary." In 1669 the nuns
removed to Brussels, and here they remained
till they left Belgium.

The community continued to flourish until
the French Revolution. When, in 1793, the
French entered Brussels, the soldiers were bil-
leted on the nuns for several days.

They ransacked the house, carrying off the
church plate and even the nuns' veils and man-
tles. In 1794, France again attacked the Neth-
erlands, and the nuns were forced to fly. They
took refuge in England and were at first established at Hartpury Court, near Gloucester, then
at Atherstone. From Atherstone the Sisters
went to Hurst Green, but finally, through the
generosity of their benefactress, the Countess of
Clare, made their home at Carisbrooke, in the
Isle of Wight. Since their establishment in this
Convent the nuns have faithfully carried out
all the observances of the Second Order—that
Order which, from the days of the Holy Patriarch St. Dominic himself, has been essentially
contemplative. They are strictly enclosed, and
devote themselves to the celebration of the
Divine Office, rising at midnight to recite Matins. They observe perpetual abstinence and fast
from Holy Cross till Easter.

There are convents of the Second Order also in Ireland, at Drogheda and Galway, and several in America.

Thus the Apostolate of Prayer goes on side by side with that of preaching, and, in the words of the Customary of the Convent of Manléon, in 1866, the Sisters "contribute, now as ever, by their prayers, their Office, their rosaries, their penances, to the success of the Fathers' ministry, and so to the salvation of souls."

"The members of the Second Order," write Father John Procter, in his Introduction to the Spirit of the Dominican Order (p. 24) "exemplify the Dominican spirit ... by an austere life of vigil, work, and contemplation. They, as Moses on the mountain, with uplifted hands, pray for the success of those who battle on the plain. Theirs is 'the better part' of Mary sitting at the feet of Jesus, pleading for those busied about much serving, that they who serve and they who are served whilst 'troubled about many things,' may not forget the 'one thing necessary.' Hidden from the world is life- long cloistered homes, these daughters of St. Dominic pray for their world; unknown to men, they offer daily penance and daily—yes, and nightly—supplication for men's salvation."

The spirit that animates the members of these cloistered retreats is well instanced by the words of Mary of Jesus, foundress of the enclosed convent of St. Catherine of Siena at Toulouse (1574–1616).

"What have you done today for the salvation of souls?" was the question with which she usually saluted her daughters. "For," says her biographer, "she richly inherited the twofold spirit of St. Dominic, and introduced into her convent the practise that every Sister should strive to gain three souls to God: one from the flames of purgatory, one from the state of sin, and one from the world to the cloister. Very often her community would fast on bread and water in order to give their dinner to the poor, and the enclosure, which was rigidly observed, did not prevent the Superior from superintending an extensive system of charity, so that the convent was always the refuge of those who were in need."[24]

In later times many convents of the Second Order began to assist more actively in the world for souls by undertaking the education of young girls and opening boarding-schools. The convents of Drogheda and Galway in Ireland are of the number.

The third division of the great Dominican family, however, embraces even a larger

number of members than does the second. It
is supposed to have been during the time of
his residence at Santa Sabina that St. Dominic instituted his Third Order, known at first
as "The Militia of Jesus Christ." "The idea of
such an Order, in which persons living in the
world should be enrolled, and those whose special duty it should be to defend the Church and
her members from the violence of the heretics,
had first suggested itself to this mind during
the labours in Languedoc." In its origin the
Third Order was essentially military, but, the
spirit and necessities of society changing, the
duties of penance and charity were substituted
for those of military service, "and something of
the sanctity of the cloister passed into family
and secular life."[25] Thence the transition to
the actual conventual life and the vows of religion was easy. Blessed Emily Bicchieri seems
to be generally regarded as the first foundress
of Conventual Tertiaries. She established a convent at Vercelli about 1255, under "the rule
of St. Augustine and the Constitutions of the
Sisters of Penance."

The Conventual Tertiaries spread rapidly
over the land, and their communities have
given to the Church, not only the great St.

25 *History of St. Dominic*, A. T. Drane, 245

Catherine de Ricci,[26] whose sanctity and miraculous life rightly entitle her to be called "one of the glories of the Order," but also multitudes of holy virgins whose memory is held in benediction and who have crowned a life of sacrifice and charity by a death most precious in the sight of the Lord.

And what, it may be asked, is the work done by these communities? What place do they hold in the organization of the Dominican Life? The writer whom we have already quoted has given a graphic description of the work of the Conventual Tertiaries: "The various Congregations supplement the Rule of the Third Order, which for communities is somewhat meagre and vague, by constitutions drawn from those of the First and Second Orders. In the Third Order we come back to the active life still informed by the spirit of contemplation, action in contemplation, and contemplation in action.... Though some congregations of Conventual Tertiaries confine themselves to a specific sphere of work, such as teaching and instructing, and duties which do not take them from their convent homes, the active work of the Third Order as an Order is not limited to a groove; theirs is

26 See *Manuel du Tiers Ordre*, R. P. Jandel, 1857.

a large and almost unlimited field. The members offer themselves 'with joy in every kind of labour for the salvation of souls and the glory of God.' Teaching in schools, whether elementary or for the higher classes, nursing the sick, either in hospitals or in their homes, reclaiming the prodigals and the Magdalens, training fatherless and motherless orphans, taking care of lepers and the plague-stricken—all these form part of the work of the Third Order, a work which they have done in the past, a work which, back at home and beyond many seas, they are still doing with devotion today. But with all and in all...to active work must be joined contemplation, the choral office, daily meditation, vocal as well as mental prayer, the Conventual Mass, devotion to Mary, visits to the Blessed Sacrament, the sacred source of 'spirit and life.'"[27]

The active work of these communities in the present day may be summed up under the heads of the education of children of all classes, the instruction of converts, and the care of the sick and infirm. The January volume for 1902 of the *Analecta Ordinis Praedicatorum* gives a list of sixteen Congregations of the "Regular

27 *Spirit of the Dominican Order*, Introduction by Father Procter, O. P., xxv.

Third Order" in the Old and New World which
have been approved by the Holy See. Many of
these comprise a large number of convents or
"branch houses." The American Congregation of
the Holy Rosary, founded in 1846, possesses
thirty-four convents, whilst that of Montelis, in
France, begun in 1846, under the same title,
numbers—or did number before the recent
destructions by the French Government—no
less than fifty-five houses.

To the Sisters of the Congregation of St.
Catherine of Siena at Etrépagny, Archbishop
Gonin, O. P., in 1868, entrusted the care of
the lepers in Trinidad, and faithfully and lov-
ingly do they continue their work amongst
the unhappy victims of that terrible disease.
In 1902 more than three hundred lepers were
being tended by this heroic community.

In the year 1842 the foundress of the first
English Congregation of Conventual Tertiaries
arrived in this country, in the humble position
of housekeeper and sacristan to Dr. Ullathorne,
who had been lately appointed to the mission
of Coventry. The Life of Mother Margaret
Hallahan, written by her spiritual daughter,
Mother Francis Raphael Drane, is probably
known to most of our readers, and need not
be given here. She had been a professed secular Tertiary in Belgium for some years before

coming to England and was a Dominican to the backbone.

When, in course of time, the excellent effects of her labours amongst the poor gave birth to the idea of founding a small religious community devoted to works of charity, it was suggested to her to join the Sisters of Mercy. "It is impossible, my lord," was her reply to Bishop Walsh; "I am a Dominican." "But," urged the Bishop, "you are alone." "If I live and die alone," she replied, "I never can be anything but a Dominican."

Mother Margaret's community began life in a corner of Dr. Ullathrone's house at Coventry but, soon afterwards, moved to a house of their own, and, gradually, amidst many difficulties and trials, the scheme took shape and matured.

In the year 1847 they were canonically erected into a religious community. The Convent of St. Dominic at Stone was founded in 1853, and, in 1877, the Constitutions were formally approved and confirmed by the Holy See.

In addition to the active works and spiritual exercises properly belonging to the Tertiary Rule, the religious of St. Catherine take upon themselves the obligation of the recitation of the Divine Office in choir, together with those monastic observances of the great Order that are suitable to their state. Besides the work

of teaching, the Sisters undertake the charge
of hospitals for incurable patients, orphanages,
visiting the sick and poor, etc. The convents of
Stoke-on-Trent, St. Mary Church and Bow, in
the east of London, belong to this Congregation.
A convent is also in the process of formation
at Hawick, in Scotland.

Mother Margaret would never allow herself
to be regarded in any sense as a *foundress.*
"There is nothing of mine in it," she would
say; "our only founder is St. Dominic." The fact
of her Community being, as to its Rule and
Constitutions, no new institute, but an inte-
gral part of one of the ancient Orders of the
Church, was the only thing about it in which
she permitted herself to glory.

The next foundation of Conventual Tertiaries in England was that of St. Rose of Lima,
at Stroud, in Gloucestershire, which began
in 1862 under the fostering care of the late
Mother Teresa Matthews. In 1886 the Congregation received the formal approbation of Rome.
Their work is much the same as that of the
Stone Congregation, and, like the latter, they
have three branch houses: Newcastle-on-Tyne,
Erdington, and Cheadle.

The Congregation of the Holy Rosary was
founded by Mother Mary Catherine Bathhurst.
Their novitiate house is at Harrow-on-the-Hill.

They have branch houses at Watford, Bognor, and Kilburn, in London.

Several other convents of Tertiaries following the Dominican Rule have of late years been established in different parts of England, Ireland, and America, and, since the dispersion of religious houses in France, many of their exiled Sisters have taken refuge and been hospitably allowed to found new homes in these three English-speaking lands.

In Australia, New Zealand, and Africa, too, English- speaking colonies of Dominican nuns are rapidly gaining ground and influence, and there are probably now few quarters of the globe where the sons and daughters of St. Dominic have not arrived with the white wool and missionary zeal of their holy founder. Of them we may say:

> There are neither speeches nor languages
> Where their voices are not heard.
> Their sound hath gone forth unto all the earth.
> And their words unto the ends of the world.

APPENDIX III
Tertiaries Living in the World

THE RELIGIOUS LIFE SHOULD not limit its action to the personal sanctification of those who are vowed to it. Its potency should pass beyond them to supernaturalise souls living outside the monastery and make them conform to the image of Christ. But how is this to be done? The founders of religious Orders have discovered a method, by establishment of what are called Third Orders, by which the fragrance of religion is wafted beyond the cloister to the great world outside.[28] "The history of this institution," says Pére Lacordaire, "is one of the fairest pages

---

28 "Those who are conversant with—indeed, who find the strength and consolation of their lives in the Acts of the Saints well know that there is not a nook of the mystical Paradise of our heavenly Spouse where the flowers grow thicker or smell more fragrantly than this Order of multitudinous child-like Saints. Nowhere in the Church does the Incarnate Word show His delight at being with the children of men in more touching simplicity, with more unearthly sweetness or more spouse-like familiarity, than on this the youngest family of St. Dominic." (Father Faber's *Blessed Sacrament*, 2nd Edition, 565, note)

of all literature. It has formed Saints in every
rank and condition of society, whose members
vie with those of the desert and the cloister.
Women especially have enriched the Third
Orders with their priceless virtues. Too often
bearing from childhood a galling yoke, they
have been made free by the girdle of St. Francis or the scapular of St. Dominic.

The convent has come to them, since they
have been unable to go to it; and in some
remote corner of their father's or husband's
house they have made themselves a hidden
sanctuary filled with the presence of the Invis-
ible Spouse, the sole object of their love. Who
has not heard of St. Catherine of Siena and
St. Rose of Lima, those two Dominicans stars
by which Europe and America have been made
bright? Who but has read of the Franciscan
St. Elizabeth of Hungary? And so God's Holy
Spirit varies His work according to the times,
proportioning His wonders to the needs of His
people; and after He has made them flourish
in the desert, He leads them out into the high-
ways of the world."

It is difficult to say which among the different Third Orders comes first chronologically.
Certainly St. Dominic instituted his after he
had founded the mother house of Dominican nuns at Prouille and the Order of Friars

Preachers.[29] "It consisted" (to quote Pére Lacordaire again) "of men and women living in the
world who undertook to defend the liberty
and property of the Church by every means
in their power. When Dominic had been canonized, the members of this association took
the name of the Cavaliers of Jesus Christ and
of St. Dominic. Later on its militant character
disappeared with the cause that gave it birth,
and the association consecrated itself to the
work of interior sanctification under the title of
St. Dominic's Brothers and Sisters of Penance."
But the memory of their primitive object shows
how whole-hearted should be their devotion to
Holy Church and how steadfast and stanch
should be their faith.

These, then, are the two characteristics of St.
Dominic's Third Order—an intense, practical
faith and a spirit of mortification. Without for-
getting that penance is but a means to the end,
the Dominican Tertiary should love to practise it according to the measure of his strength.
He should find the surest help in his spiritual
life, not so much in works of extraordinary

29 "A complaint of the clergy of England was laid before
Henry III of England in 1255 against the Friars Preachers and Minors. *They have devised new confraternities into
which men and women enter in such numbers that scarcely
can anyone be found who does not belong to them.*" (Father
Conway, O. P., *Dominican Order*, 23)

austerities, as by depriving himself of whatsoever serves only to pamper the flesh.

As for the advantages of belonging to the Third Order, they are beyond number. The Tertiary is a true member of the Order of St. Dominic, and, in consequence, participates in all the merits of the Order accumulated through seven centuries—in the merits, that is, of our holy founder, of our great Saints, of all our beatified brethren—that vast multitude that no man can number. Said Benedict XIII: "If one should wish to celebrate each Dominican Saint on a day apart, he must lengthen the year"; and when someone asked him the number of Saints in the Order of Friars Preachers, he answered simply: "Count, if you can, all the stars of Heaven." And this vast treasury of merit is added to day by day by the unending labours of apostles and the penances of holy virgins.

Again, Tertiaries have part in all the indulgences with which the Popes have enriched the Order of St. Dominic. Besides this, there is a special list proper to the Tertiaries alone. Finally, they communicate in all the indulgences and privileges of every other Third Order. What a wealth of grace for a soul that wishes to be conformed to the image of God's Son!

Moreover, the Rule of the Third Order does not bind under sin nor by vow. Its regulations do not overburden life, nor form any real obstacle to the observance of the social duties of one's state. To know the principal obligations, one has only to write to any Dominican Father.[30] Where many Tertiaries can be grouped together, they are formed into a Chapter. The advantages of this are self-evident. But even an isolated Tertiary lives in a real community of thought and prayer and sacrifice with his Brothers and Sisters of the Order of St. Dominic. What joy, then, is his! How the weary pilgrimage of this, his exile, seems less hard to bear when it is cheered by friendly love on every side and by the firm hope and trust of being met at his journey's end and welcomed into the home of God by St. Dominic and his host of glorious children!

---

30 See the Dominican Tertiaries' *Daily Manual*, by Father Procter, O. P. (Kegan Paul, Trübner, and Co.). This manual contains a summary of the Rule, the Office of Our Lady, and the Office of the Dead, according to the Dominican rite and the formulary of the Third Order.

www.ingramcontent.com/pod-product-compliance
Lightning Source LLC
Chambersburg PA
CBHW031448120626